The Joint Free Public Library
of
Morristown and Morris Township

THE UNTAMED WORLD

Jaguars

E. Melanie Watt

RSVP

RAINTREE
STECK-VAUGHN
P U B L I S H E R S
The Steck-Vaughn Company

Austin, Texas

Copyright © 1998 Weigl Educational Publishers Limited

All rights reserved. No part of the material protected by this copyright may be reproduced or utilized in any form or by any means, electronic or mechanical, including photocopying, recording, or by any information storage and retrieval system, without permission in writing from the copyright owner. Requests for permission to make copies of any part of the work should be mailed to: Copyright Permissions, Steck-Vaughn Company, P.O. Box 26015, Austin, TX 78755.

Published by Raintree Steck-Vaughn Publishers, an imprint of Steck-Vaughn Company.

Library of Congress Cataloguing-in-Publication Data

Watt, Melanie

    Jaguars/E. Melanie Watt

        p.   cm. -- (The untamed world)

    Includes bibliographical references (p. 63) and index.

    Summary: Describes the physical characteristics, classification, behaviour, habitat, and endangered status of the jaguar.

    ISBN 0-8172-4568-5

    1. Jaguar--Juvenile literature.   [1. Jaguar. 2. Endangered species.] I. Title. II. Series.

QL737.C23W38 1998

599.755--dc21

                         97-9064

                            CIP

                            AC

Printed and bound in Canada

1234567890 01 00 99 98 97

Project Editor
Lauri Seidlitz

Design and Illustration
Warren Clark

Raintree Steck-Vaughn Publishers Editor
Kathy DeVico

Copy Editors
Janice Parker
Leslie Strudwick

Layout
Chris Bowerman

About the Author
As part of a two-year research project on jaguars, Dr. Melanie Watt spent 8 months tracking the big cat in the tropical forests of Belize, Central America. She has written numerous articles about jaguars and is also author of the book *Jaguar Woman*.

Acknowledgments
The publisher wishes to thank Warren Rylands for inspiring this series.

Photograph Credits

Frank S. Balthis: page 33; **Corel Corporation**: cover, pages 4, 5, 6, 7 right, 10, 18, 23, 26, 27, 40, 59, 60, 61; **Tom Myers**: page 20; **Tom Stack and Associates**: pages 25 (Warren Garst), 37 (Wendy Shattil/Bob Rozinski), 38 (Mary Clay); **Dave Taylor**: page 29; **U.S. Fish and Wildlife Service**: page 11 (Ron Singer); **Visuals Unlimited**: pages 17, 21 (James Beveridge); **E. Melanie Watt**: pages 7 left, 12, 13, 15, 16, 19 bottom left, 19 top right, 22, 24, 28, 30, 32, 34, 36, 39, 41, 43, 44, 52, 53, 54, 56, 57.

Every reasonable effort has been made to trace ownership and to obtain permission to reprint copyright material. The publishers would be pleased to have any errors or omissions brought to their attention so that they may be corrected in subsequent printings.

Contents

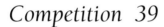

Introduction

Jaguars often live in swampy, thick, tropical forests.

People sometimes think that jaguars are vicious beasts that live only in the deepest jungles of South America. In fact, jaguars can be found in North and Central America, as well as in South America. Few people know much about jaguars. They are one of the least studied of the world's big cats. Jaguars often live in swampy, thick, tropical forests. This makes seeing them very difficult and studying them even harder.

Recently, biologists have learned more about jaguars. This book will show you what they have discovered. Once you read this book, you will be one of the few people who understands the life and legends that surround one of the world's most beautiful and reclusive cats.

Opposite: Despite its heavy weight, a jaguar can climb very well and can drag heavy prey into trees.

A jaguar is a powerful hunter.

Features

Jaguars and leopards are easy to tell apart in the wild because they live on different continents.

Opposite: Jaguars have been hunted near extinction because of their beautiful fur.

Most people cannot tell jaguars and leopards apart. Once you know what to look for, however, it is easy to tell one from the other. Jaguars are usually bigger than leopards. They have shorter tails and heavier bodies. Jaguars also have bigger heads, shorter legs, and bigger paws compared to their bodies. These differences make jaguars look more compact and powerful, but less graceful than leopards.

Another way to tell a jaguar from a leopard is from the spots on its fur. Both cats have black-outlined circles, called **rosettes**, on their coats. Jaguars' rosettes are usually larger. They often have one or more dots in the center. Leopards' rosettes are smaller and usually empty. Jaguars and leopards are easy to tell apart in the wild because they live on different continents.

A jaguar's rosettes (left) are larger than a leopard's rosettes (right). Jaguar rosettes often have dots in the center.

Classification

All cat species have many similarities. Cats have rounded heads, strong, compact bodies, whiskers, large eyes, and curved, sharp claws. All cats can hear, see, and smell very well. They also have a good sense of balance. There are about 36 species of wild cats in the world. Of these, some are considered small cats and some are considered large cats.

Scientists classify most of the small cats in one group. Jaguars are thought to be closely related to leopards, lions, and tigers. These species of big cats are grouped together. Cheetahs are also sometimes considered a big cat species. They are in a special group all their own. The relationships between big cats are reflected in their scientific names. Every known species and subspecies of animal has a scientific, or Latin, name. This means that scientists from all over the world will understand exactly which animal another scientist is discussing, even if they speak different languages. The scientific names of jaguars, leopards, lions, and tigers all begin with *Panthera*. The scientific name of cheetahs begins with *Acinonyx*.

BIG CAT CHARACTERISTICS

*Like jaguars and leopards, lions and tigers have powerful bodies and sturdy legs. They also all have large paws with fully **retractable claws**.*

Cheetahs are smaller than jaguars. They also have smaller heads and sleeker bodies. Cheetahs have small paws and can only partially retract their claws.

Species

Ancestors of the jaguar were about 20 percent bigger than jaguars today. These animals may have been bigger because they had larger prey to eat. Fossil remains of these extra-large jaguars have been found much farther north than where jaguars now roam. Some of the fossils have even been found as far north as the Canada-United States border. There is only one species of jaguar in the world. Scientists divide living jaguars into several subspecies that live in North, South, and Central America. Another large cat, the cougar, or mountain lion, also lives in the Americas. However, jaguars and cougars are not thought to be closely related.

SUBSPECIES

The Latin name used for all jaguars is *Panthera onca*. Each word following *Panthera onca* is different for each subspecies. Biologists have divided jaguars into eight subspecies. Each subspecies lives in a different part of the jaguar's range. The following list gives the common and Latin names for the eight jaguar subspecies:

Common Name	Latin Name	Status
Arizona jaguar	*Panthera onca arizonensis*	extinct
Eastern Mexican jaguar	*Panthera onca veraecrucis*	close to extinction
Western Mexican jaguar	*Panthera onca hernandesii*	very reduced numbers
Yucatan jaguar	*Panthera onca goldmani*	reduced range
Panama jaguar	*Panthera onca centralis*	very reduced numbers
Peruvian jaguar	*Panthera onca peruviana*	reduced range
Amazon jaguar	*Panthera onca onca*	reduced range
Pantanal jaguar	*Panthera onca paraguensis*	isolated populations

Size

Jaguars are the third largest cat in the world. Only lions and tigers are bigger. Leopards, cougars, and cheetahs are all smaller than jaguars. The size of a particular jaguar depends on where it lives, what it eats, whether it is a male or female, and its age. Jaguars in Central America tend to be smaller than those in Brazil. Jaguars stand about 27 to 29.5 inches (68 to 75 cm) high at the shoulders. Their tails are less than one-third of their body length. Including their tails, female jaguars are usually about 5 to 7.2 feet (1.6 to 2.2 m) long and weigh 93 to 168 pounds (42 to 76 kg). This is about 11 times larger than the average domestic cat. Male jaguars are about 10 to 20 percent bigger than females. Males are usually 5.6 to 7.9 feet (1.7 to 2.4 m) long. They normally weigh from 126 to 220 pounds (57 to 100 kg). One of the heaviest jaguars ever recorded was a male that weighed 348 pounds (158 kg).

The only cats bigger than jaguars are lions and tigers.

LIFE SPAN

The life span of a jaguar in the wild is about 11 to 12 years. Jaguars in captivity can live for more than 20 years. One female in captivity was reported to have lived to be 32 years old. Older jaguars may have worn or missing teeth, or infections. They may not be able to move as quickly as younger cats. In captivity this is usually not a problem, but if their hunting skills fail in the wild, jaguars will not survive. Veterinary care in captivity also helps increase a jaguar's life span.

Fur

Most jaguars have a golden coat that fades to white on their cheeks, throat, belly, and parts of their legs. All jaguars have rosettes as well as other spots of various sizes and shapes. The markings are larger on a jaguar's shoulders and back than on its head, neck, and legs. No two jaguars have the same pattern of spots. Even the two sides of one jaguar have different markings. Not all jaguars have a golden coat. Some jaguars are **melanistic**, or black. Although these jaguars look completely black, when they stand in the light, you can see rosettes and other spots. There are also albino, or white, jaguars, but these are extremely rare. Young jaguars tend to have bushier fur. When jaguars get very old, their fur becomes thinner and lighter in color.

Even black jaguars have spots. The rosettes and other markings are just harder to see.

Special Adaptations

Jaguars have many features that help them survive the challenges of their environment.

Hearing

Like other cat species, jaguars hear very well. They use this sense when hunting to locate their prey. The sense of hearing is very important for jaguars. They must be able to sneak up on their prey without being seen. Just by hearing its prey's movement noises, a jaguar can creep silently toward it without being seen.

Sight

Compared to other meat-eaters, cats have the biggest eyes. Jaguars, like other cats, can see in color. They use their well-developed sense of sight to help find their prey. They can see well during the day and night. Their eyes adjust very quickly to sudden darkness. This makes it easier for them to hunt when stalking through the undergrowth. They can also judge distances extremely well. This is very important in order for them to successfully pounce on their prey.

Smell

The jaguar's sense of smell is good, but it is not as important for hunting as its senses of hearing or sight. A jaguar's sense of smell may help it find prey. It is also important in interactions with other jaguars. Jaguars sniff **scent marks** left by other cats. These marks help a jaguar tell which other jaguars have recently been in its **home range**. It can use this information to avoid an area that is being used by another jaguar. This helps it avoid direct confrontations. From a scent mark, a jaguar can also likely tell the sex of another jaguar and whether it is ready to breed. It can use this scent information to find mates.

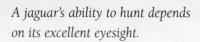

A jaguar's ability to hunt depends on its excellent eyesight.

Teeth

Jaguars have 30 teeth and very powerful jaws. Compared to the size of their other teeth, their canine teeth are huge. These large teeth are used to hold on to and kill their prey. The smaller teeth are used to help chew meat.

Whiskers

The whiskers of a jaguar are very well developed. These whiskers have nerve endings. Jaguars use them to "feel" whatever they are touching. This makes it much easier for jaguars to travel through thick bush and follow their prey at night.

Tongue

The jaguar's tongue is covered with rough bumps that point toward the back of its mouth. Jaguars use their tongue to clean their fur and to drink water. The bumps help the cat scoop up liquid. This rough surface also helps a jaguar clean the last bits of meat off bones when they eat.

---

*With its strong teeth and powerful jaws, a jaguar can easily crush the shell of a turtle and chew through the tough skin of a **caiman**.*

More Special Adaptations

Legs

Jaguars have short, powerful legs. They are not designed to run long distances, but to pounce on their prey from relatively short distances. A jaguar often uses its strong legs to drag its food a long way from the kill site. Jaguars also use their legs for swimming. They are very good swimmers and are often found near water.

Paws

In most cases you can tell the tracks made by cats from those made by dogs. Dogs have claws that are permanently in the outstretched position. Like most other cats, jaguars have retractable claws, meaning they keep their claws in except when they are using them. Dog tracks have a small dot on the ground above each toe. Cats usually keep their claws pulled in while they walk, so they leave no claw marks. All cats use their claws to defend themselves and to hold on to their prey. The claws are always very sharp, in part because they do not touch the ground and wear down while they walk. Their feet are covered with hair, except for the pads on the bottom. This helps them follow their prey silently.

Tail

A jaguar uses its tail to help balance itself while climbing. As with other cat species, the tail is also a good way of telling a jaguar's mood. A nonmoving tail tends to indicate that the cat is relaxed. A rapidly swishing tail is a warning sign that the jaguar is feeling anxious.

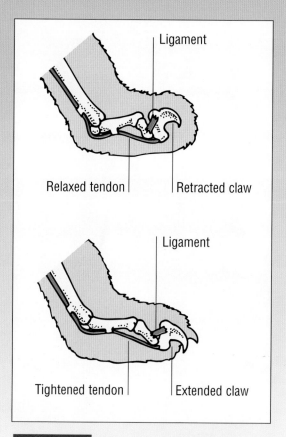

A cat's claws stay sharp partly because it keeps them retracted until it needs them.

A Jaguar Quiz

Try this quiz to see how much you know about jaguars.
Are the following statements true or false? The answers are
at the bottom of this page.

1. Jaguars are the second biggest cat in the world.

2. Black and golden jaguars are different subspecies.

3. Leopards look more graceful than jaguars.

4. In the wild, jaguars are found only in South America.

5. A jaguar with a swishing tail is probably agitated.

6. The jaguar's ancestors were bigger than the jaguars of today.

1) False. Tigers and lions are both bigger than jaguars.

2) False. Even jaguars that are brothers and sisters can be different colors.

3) True. With longer legs and tails, leopards more graceful than living jaguars.

4) False. Jaguars are also found in Central America and Mexico.

5) True. Jaguars, like house cats, will swish their tails when they are anxious.

6) True. The ancestors of jaguars were about 20 percent bigger than living jaguars.

Social Activities

Jaguars rarely fight with other jaguars.

Opposite: A jaguar spends most of its life alone.

Jaguars spend most of the time living alone. A male and female jaguar might travel together for a short time during their mating period. They will return to their solitary lifestyle after mating. Cubs stay with their mother for up to two years. When they can take care of themselves, they leave to live on their own. Sometimes cubs from the same litter will live together for a short time after they leave their mother. Jaguars rarely fight with other jaguars. They seem to avoid one another and find mates by communicating from a distance.

Except during mating, or in zoos, it is rare for adult jaguars to spend time with one another.

Communication

Jaguars have many ways of communicating with one another. This communication is usually not face-to-face. They most often send and receive information from a distance.

Body Language

Jaguars behave in much the same way as other big cats when they are aggressive or defensive. If they are defensive, or submissive, their ears flatten back tightly against their heads. Their pupils enlarge, and they often flatten themselves against the ground or back away low to the ground. They may even roll over on their backs. When they are on the offensive, they behave in just the opposite way. They hold their ears forward and stand up with their weight mostly on their front legs. When adult male and female jaguars are being friendly toward each other, they sometimes rub their necks together. This usually happens only when the jaguars are mating.

This jaguar is taking a defensive pose.

Markings

Some jaguars flatten grass and other vegetation to make bedding sites. They may mark these areas on trails by urinating to leave scent marks. Jaguars also make **scrapes**. These are places where they scrape up a patch of earth with their paws. Sometimes they mark a scrape with droppings or with urine. Jaguars also sometimes rake, or scratch, tree trunks. Scrapes and scratches on trees are thought to be a way of communicating with other cats. Jaguars are not the only big cats to scratch tree trunks. Cougars, tigers, and leopards also rake tree trunks with their claws.

Scientists measure jaguar scrapes to help them guess the size of jaguars in the area.

Sounds

Some people describe jaguar vocalizations as sounding more like coughs than roars. They compare jaguar sounds to snoring noises. A jaguar usually makes three or more short, hoarse coughs in a row. Since the sounds travel a long way, jaguars tend to sound closer than they really are when they make these calls.

Researchers report that the calls of adult females sound slightly different from those of adult males. They could not tell the difference between the calls of young male jaguars and those of adult females. A female often calls when she is searching for a mate. A male answers back until they find each other. Hunters often imitate these calls in order to attract or locate jaguars.

This jaguar is vocalizing as it walks.

Jaguar Cubs

Throughout her life, a female jaguar will probably not have more than eight or nine cubs.

Opposite: Cubs are over two weeks old when they take their first steps.

Jaguar cubs are small and fragile when they are born, but they soon become playful and curious about their world. For up to 2 years, their mother will protect the cubs and feed them. She will also teach them the hunting and other skills they need to survive on their own. When the young are old enough, they leave their mother and find their own territories. Only then does the mother mate again and raise other cubs. Throughout her life, a female jaguar will probably not have more than eight or nine cubs. The cubs will not produce young of their own until they are about three years old.

Cubs stay with their mothers for up to 2 years.

Birth

The male and female jaguar are only together briefly during mating. The **gestation period** for jaguars is about 13 weeks long. There are usually two cubs in a litter, but there can be one to three cubs born. Very rarely a litter will have four cubs. Jaguar cubs, like kittens, are usually born with their eyes shut. When very young, the cubs have long, bushy, spotted coats. As jaguar cubs get older, their small spots grow larger, and some spots develop into rosettes. Cubs that are born with a light golden coat darken slightly in color as they age. Black and golden jaguars were once thought to be different subspecies. Now scientists know that they are not, since they can both be found in the same litter.

Jaguars born with a black coat stay black all their lives.

Care

The father jaguar has no contact with the young. The mother jaguar gives birth to the cubs alone and raises them all by herself. The mother often hides her cubs in a den until they are about two months old. The den may be in bushes or other vegetation, in a cave, between rocks, under a fallen log, under burrowed out tree roots, or under a

A jaguar near its den

riverbank. She hunts near the den until the cubs are old enough to travel. Like most mammals, jaguar mothers are very protective of their young. They will defend their cubs against anything that might try to harm them. Young jaguars are occasionally killed by large snakes or by caimans.

A mother will not let other jaguars near her cubs, not even the cubs' father. Although it is rare, there have been reports of male jaguars killing jaguar cubs. One large jaguar was found to have eaten two small jaguar cubs.

Although male lions often kill other lions' cubs, male jaguars rarely kill jaguar cubs. One reason for this difference is that lions live in social groups called prides. When a male lion joins a new pride, none of the cubs are his. Unless he kills the cubs, he will be helping to raise his competitor's cubs. The lionesses in his new pride will also be able to produce his own cubs faster if they do not have to raise another male's cubs. Male jaguars do not help protect the adult female or raise the young, so they will never "waste" their energy raising another jaguar's cubs. If they were to kill cubs, they might accidentally kill one of their own.

Development

Birth – 5 Weeks

Small and helpless at birth, jaguar cubs are about 16 inches (40 cm) long and weigh about 28 ounces (800 g). For the first few days after the cubs are born, the mother rarely leaves the den. The cubs cannot even mew at this age. Instead they make bleating noises, similar to the sounds a sheep might make.

The cubs grow quickly, gaining about 1.7 ounces (48 g) per day for the first 50 days. The cubs are usually born with their eyes closed, opening them after about 8 days. The cubs first walk at about 18 days of age.

6 – 10 Weeks

The cubs are able to follow their mother when they are between six and eight weeks old. They remain in the den for about 8 weeks. By this time, the cubs have developed good climbing skills. When the cubs are about ten weeks old, they begin to eat meat, but they will continue to drink their mother's milk for several more months.

For cubs, playing is a way to learn hunting and survival skills. Cubs often play with teeth and claws extended.

Although young cubs have not developed their hunting skills, their instincts make them curious about their environment.

11 – 15 Weeks

The cubs continue to play and explore. This helps to improve their coordination and other skills that they will eventually need to hunt successfully. At about 15 weeks, the cubs' bleating cries turn into mewing sounds. Their calls get deeper with age until they are about one year old, when they begin to sound like adults.

16 – 20 Weeks

Near the end of this period, the cubs drink much less of their mother's milk and eat mostly meat. By their seventh month, the spots and colors of their coats lose their cublike look and become their permanent adult markings.

Habitat

Jaguars are usually found in places that have plant cover, water, and lots of other animals for them to eat.

Opposite: A jaguar is always watching for prey—in trees, on the ground, and in water.

Jaguars spend a lot of time near the water. They are excellent swimmers.

Jaguars can live in many different types of habitats, including rain forest, marshland, and even floating islands of vegetation. They are usually found in places that have plant cover, water, and lots of other animals for them to eat. Although they spend much of their time near rivers, swamps, or other bodies of water, they are quite adaptable. Jaguars have been seen in deserts and on mountains at an altitude higher than 8,859 feet (2,700 m) above sea level.

One of the reasons that jaguars may be able to use such different habitats is that they can eat many types of animals. Their prey animals include different species of mammals, reptiles, and birds, which live in many different types of habitats. Jaguars tend to do best in places where there are few or no humans. Many people are afraid of jaguars. Some people try to kill any jaguars they see.

Jaguar Territories

Within its territory, or home range, a jaguar eats, finds mates, and interacts with other jaguars. The size of the home range depends on the habitat. Some parts of a larger home range might not be used much, such as a lake, where jaguars would mainly use the banks and the shallow waters. The size of the home range also depends on how many and what types of prey are available. Larger home ranges are found in areas where prey is less common. In these cases, the jaguar needs a larger area to search for prey.

Female jaguars raise their young within a home range that is usually at least 10 to 15 square miles (25 to 38 sq km). The home ranges of male jaguars are twice this size. The home range of a male jaguar often overlaps the home ranges of one or more females. Except during mating, jaguars are able to avoid one another by long-distance communication. In this way they can use the same areas, but at different times.

A jaguar's rosettes provide excellent camouflage in the jungle forests.

Jaguars often rest during midday heat, but hunt both in daylight and in darkness.

Seasonal Activities

There are usually two main seasons in jaguar habitats: the rainy season and the dry season. In the rainy season, areas of a jaguar's territory may not be usable because of flooding. This means that many jaguars have much smaller territories during the rainy season. The jaguar's prey is also often crowded into these smaller areas at this time of year. This makes them easier to find. Jaguar eating habits change throughout the year. Some foods, such as turtle or iguana eggs, are available only in one season. Some of the jaguar's prey may be easier to catch in a particular season. For example, during sea turtle nesting season, the turtles are easy to catch when they climb out of the water to lay their eggs on the beach. Many prey species tend to have young in one season and not in the other. Some jaguar prey may also be easier to catch when they are protecting their young. For larger prey, jaguars may even prefer hunting the young.

On the Track of a Jaguar

Some people spend their entire lives living in or near jaguar home ranges yet never see one of these big cats. The jaguar's senses of smell, sight, and hearing are so good that it will almost always sense people before being seen. Even in areas where jaguar tracks constantly mark the trails, these big cats may seem invisible. If you are in an area where jaguars are known to live, try looking for these signs that they often leave behind:

1. Tracks may be found that are like those of house cats, except they are much bigger. Jaguar tracks are usually 3 to 5 inches (8 to 13 cm) across and have four toe prints. There are not normally any nail marks above the toes.

2. **Scat**, or feces, is often found along trails. It usually contains a lot of hair and bones from the jaguar's prey. Jaguars eat many different species, so the scat may also contain armadillo scutes (bony plates), feathers, scales, or eggshells.

3. Scrapes may be found along trails. These scrape marks are usually about 14.5 inches long by 4 inches wide (37 by 10 cm).

4. Scratch marks on trees may be seen in some jaguar areas. Look for claw scratches that are usually between 16 inches (40 cm) and 6 feet (1.8 m) from the ground.

5. Bedding areas may be seen at 550-yard (500-m) intervals along the trail. These areas of flattened vegetation are about 3.3 by 1.6 feet (1 by .5 m) in size.

Scientists discover a lot about what jaguars eat by examining their scat.

Wildlife Biologists Talk About Jaguars

Louise Emmons

"The jaguar...is now threatened not only by skin hunters and habitat destruction, but also by the extinction of many of its prey, every species of which is intensively hunted by humans."

Louise Emmons is a biologist who has spent years studying jaguars, cougars, and ocelots in the rain forests of Peru.

Rafael Hoogesteijn

"If we do not preserve jaguars, they will be converted like our rain forests and finally ourselves, into dust and smoke."

Rafael Hoogesteijn is a veterinarian and a zoologist who has long been involved in research on jaguars in Venezuela. He is coauthor of a book titled *The Jaguar*.

Peter G. Crawshaw, Jr.

"With each passing year, the forests that shelter and protect these magnificent beasts shrink further and further before man's relentless encroachment."

Peter G. Crawshaw, Jr., is a biologist who has spent years studying jaguars and other wildlife in the Pantanal, an area in southwestern Brazil.

Food

Although jaguars are large, many of the animals they prey upon are relatively small.

Opposite: A jaguar's sturdy body is ideal for hunting in the forest.

Jaguars are **carnivores**, which means that the flesh of other animals is their main source of food. They also eat a small amount of vegetation, including grass. There is even a report of a jaguar eating avocados! Although jaguars are large, many of the animals they prey upon are relatively small. Most of their prey are animals that weigh more than 2.2 pounds (1 kg). They also eat even smaller animals. Their diet changes, depending on what prey are available in their territories. This depends on where a jaguar lives. The diet of the jaguar also changes depending on the season. Jaguars are not always successful in their hunts. Occasionally a jaguar may even be hurt or killed while hunting.

This jaguar is eating a bird it has hunted and caught.

What They Eat

Jaguars are **opportunistic feeders**. This means they eat almost any reasonably sized animal they come across. Jaguars have been reported to eat more than 85 different prey species, including mammals, reptiles, birds, and fish. Some of their favorite mammal prey are armadillos, pacas, agoutis, and peccaries. One of the jaguar's favorite foods in South America is an animal called the capybara. Capybaras are the world's largest living rodents. They look a bit like huge guinea pigs with longer legs. They can weigh up to 174 pounds (79 kg). Capybaras can make up a large part of the jaguar's diet in South America. However, capybaras are not found in all parts of the jaguar's range. Jaguars in other areas must eat more of other species.

Jaguars eat many species of reptiles. Their favorite reptile prey include caimans, turtles, and iguanas. Jaguars also eat reptile eggs, such as those of the iguana and caiman.

Some other animals that jaguars eat are a bit surprising. Scientists have found evidence that jaguars have eaten frogs, porcupines, skunks, and snakes, as well as dolphins and stingrays.

In South America, capybaras are one of the jaguar's favorite foods.

Jaguar Foods

Although jaguars usually kill their own food, they will also eat carrion, or dead animals, if they encounter them. What an individual jaguar eats depends on what it finds while hunting. It may also depend on what the jaguar has become accustomed to eating or is good at catching. A jaguar's diet is likely to change with the season and with its age. Young jaguars might not be as skilled at catching larger or more difficult prey.

Pacas

Birds

Armadillos

Iguanas

Fish

Peccaries

Carrion

How They Hunt

Jaguars hunt alone. They use their senses of hearing, sight, and smell to locate their prey. Jaguars are not long-distance runners. They tend to lie in wait or quietly stalk and then ambush their prey from short distances. Because they eat so many different species, they use a variety of hunting techniques, depending on their prey.

Catching Their Prey

Jaguars often scoop fish out of the water with their paws. To catch turtles, jaguars usually turn them over on their backs. Then they scoop their bodies out of the shells. Jaguars may pounce and kill large prey, such as the capybara, with a bite to the back of the head. A jaguar may also kill its prey by simply hitting it hard on the head with a front paw. Unlike tigers, jaguars rarely kill by biting the throats of their prey. Jaguars are powerful hunters. They kill caimans and other reptiles both in and out of the water. Jaguars have been reported killing 6-foot (1.8-m) long caimans and 9.8-foot (3-m) long anacondas.

Jaguars' large paws allow them to move silently through forest undergrowth. This helps them to sneak up on prey.

Even though they usually hunt smaller animals, jaguars can also kill full-grown cows, horses, and tapir. Tapir can weigh as much as 573 pounds (260 kg). For these very large prey, jaguars may bite the neck or pull the head around with their paws, pulling the prey off balance and taking them to the ground. Often these large prey will break their necks in the fall.

Once it has killed its prey, a jaguar will often drag the body a long way to a protected area to eat. It may even drag very large prey away from the kill site. People have observed jaguars dragging full-grown horses and cows more than 650 yards (600 m). Though not nearly as common, jaguars will sometimes carry cows or horses up into trees to eat them.

A jaguar depends on the element of surprise to ambush its prey.

Competition

Jaguars may be hurt during a hunt when they are stabbed, scratched, or bitten, or when they are trampled by larger prey.

E ven though jaguars are big, powerful predators, they do not always win their competitions. Jaguars may be hurt during a hunt when they are stabbed, scratched, or bitten, or when they are trampled by larger prey. Jaguars that hunt poisonous snakes or porcupines can also have obvious problems.

Opposite: Although jaguars are fierce hunters, they do not always catch their prey.

Jaguars and people share some of the same food preferences, so jaguars that live farthest from humans may also have a better choice of food. Iguanas are a popular food enjoyed by both jaguars and humans in Latin America.

Competing with Other Jaguars

Jaguars rarely fight with or kill other jaguars. They usually avoid one another as much as possible. Jaguars communicate over long distances by roaring, and by leaving scent or scrape marks. In very rare cases, however, jaguars have eaten other jaguars. Why or when they might do this is unknown. Scientists know it has happened because a few males that have been killed were found to have other jaguars' remains in their stomachs.

Competing with Other Species

In every country that jaguars live, cougars can also be found. Even though cougars are likely to compete for some of the same prey as jaguars, the two species seem to avoid one another. There is some evidence that jaguars will attack and kill cougars. This is not very common, but it does happen occasionally. Cougars and jaguars may avoid conflicts simply because of the types of areas that they each prefer. Jaguars tend to spend much of their time near, or even in, water. Cougars seem to prefer drier home ranges.

Although the cougar and jaguar sometimes live in the same areas, they rarely fight.

Competing with Humans

Humans are by far the biggest threat to jaguars. In some countries, jaguars are not protected by law. This often means that jaguars are shot on sight. People sometimes shoot jaguars because they are afraid of them. However, jaguars are the only big cats that do not become man-eaters, so they are not a real threat. Other people shoot jaguars because they want their skins. In most areas, jaguar skins can no longer be legally traded because jaguars are protected by laws. Some people kill jaguars because they are trying to protect their **domestic animals**. While jaguars sometimes kill cattle, they are responsible for only a very small percentage of all cattle deaths. Many more cows die from disease or starvation, while others drown in floods or are killed by other predators. Humans may even cause jaguars to hunt domestic animals by overhunting many of the prey species that jaguars prefer. Human hunting may diminish the numbers of a jaguar's normal prey species. When this happens, the jaguar must switch to other prey, which may include cattle or other livestock.

Jaguars are sometimes killed by people protecting their cattle. As cattle farms take up more jaguar territory, conflicts between humans and jaguars are increasing.

Folklore

Jaguars were common in the folklore and religion of Central and South American Aboriginal cultures. Jaguars were worshiped by cultures that include the Aztec, Maya, Olmec, and Zapotec. For many of these peoples, jaguars meant terror and mystery, but also strength, nobility, and bravery. Jaguars were also thought to have magical and healing powers.

The Guayaki of Paraguay still greatly fear jaguars. This is shown in much of their folklore. Many of their taboos involve jaguars attacking them if they disobey rules. For example, they believe that a person who does not share his food with his friends will be mauled by a jaguar.

Opposite: The Mayan word for "jaguar" also means "priest." The jaguar priest is a common image in ancient Mayan artwork.

This is a modern statue of a jaguar that stands outside a Mexican hotel. The jaguar remains a popular image for artists.

Folklore History

In the Mayan religion, the god who rules the world is a jaguar. The Mayan word for "jaguar," *balam*, can also mean "priest." The Temple of the Giant Jaguar in Tikal, Guatemala, was built by the Maya about 1,300 years ago. The Maya believed that solar eclipses were caused by the jaguar eating the sun.

In the Aztec religion, several gods, including the god of the night sky and the rain god, were represented as jaguars. The best Aztec warriors belonged to either the order of the eagle or the order of the jaguar.

Jaguars played an even more important role in the Olmec culture. The Olmec formed a jaguar cult. Their art often showed "were-jaguars," creatures that were half-human and half-jaguar. The Olmec were said to have deformed their own heads to make themselves look more like jaguars.

Temple of the Giant Jaguar in Tikal, Guatemala

Folktales

In folktales jaguars can be helpful, dangerous, or even misunderstood. They are usually seen as great hunters. In many tales the jaguar is seen as a magical part of the night jungle. Ancient tales also tell of jaguars that are mystical and can become half-human/half-jaguar creatures. Books that include jaguar folktales are often difficult to find because many Mayan stories were not written down. Many tales are told and retold and change with each retelling.

Jaguars as Hunters

"The Possum and the Jaguar" is a Mayan fable about a young possum that chooses a jaguar to be his godfather. The possum then tries to live like a jaguar, with disastrous results.

Monejo, Victor, translated by Wallace Kaufman. *The Bird Who Cleans the World and Other Mayan Fables*. Connecticut: Curbstone Press, 1991.

"The Deer and the Jaguar Share a House" is a Brazilian folktale that explains why deer and jaguars cannot live together. In this story, a deer and a jaguar build a house and live in it together, until the deer discovers more about the jaguar's diet.

Best-Loved Folktales of the World. Selected and introduced by Joanna Cole. New York: Anchor Press/Doubleday, 1982.

Dangerous Jaguars

"The Great Jaguar" is a Mayan fable about two hunters who find a jaguar. The moral of the story is that people should avoid unnecessary dangers, especially those as great as hunting a jaguar.

Monejo, Victor, translated by Wallace Kaufman. *The Bird Who Cleans the World and Other Mayan Fables*. Connecticut: Curbstone Press, 1991.

More Folktales

Helpful Jaguars

"**The Old One's Friendship: the Dog, the Jaguar, and the Coyote**" is a Mayan tale about three aging animals that join together to hunt. The coyote cheats the other two and is thrown out of the group, but the old dog and the old jaguar decide to travel together and help each other.

Monejo, Victor, translated by Wallace Kaufman. *The Bird Who Cleans the World and Other Mayan Fables*. Connecticut: Curbstone Press, 1991.

Jaguar Creation

"**The Myth of the Jaguar**" explains how the jaguar was created. In this poem, the jaguar's skin was created from moss, its movements were created by the wind, its hair from light and shadow, and its eyes by lightning.

Cuadra, Pablo Antonio, translated by Steven F. White. *The Birth of the Sun: Selected Poems*. Greensboro: Unicorn Press, 1988.

Journey of the Nightly Jaguar tells how each night, the sun turns into a jaguar that travels through the jungle until dawn, when it once again changes back into the sun. The illustrations and poetry were inspired by drawings on an ancient Mayan urn.

Burton, Albert. *Journey of the Nightly Jaguar*. New York: Simon and Schuster, 1996.

Mystical Jaguars

Heart of a Jaguar is about a young Mayan boy's struggle and sacrifice to save his village. Balam is frightened of the jaguar, after whom he was named. Despite his fear, he believes the jaguar is an important part of his world. This novel blends ancient Mayan folklore and history to give an inside look at the life and death struggles of the ancient Maya.

Talbert, Marc. *Heart of a Jaguar.* New York: Simon and
    Schuster, 1995.

"When Jaguars Ate the Moon" is a South American tale explaining how jaguars cause eclipses by eating the moon. It explains that some people make a lot of noise and even fire off guns during eclipses to scare the jaguars away from the moon.

Brusca, Maria Christina and Wilson, Tona. *When
    Jaguars Ate the Moon and Other Stories About Animals
    and Plants of the Americas.* New York: Henry Holt and
    Co. Inc., 1995.

Myths vs. Facts

Jaguars often stalk humans.

Jaguars follow humans and other animals that travel through their territories. This tendency led to the belief that jaguars were a danger to humans. Out of fear, hunters would often try to double back and kill the jaguar following their group. Many researchers have also reported being followed while they were following jaguar tracks. Jaguars tend to stop following a particular person if he or she is often in the area. Their tendency to follow most likely means that jaguars are just curious about anything new in their territories.

Jaguars are man-eaters.

Man-eaters are animals that regularly kill and eat humans. Although jaguars are often feared by humans, they are much less likely to kill humans than are tigers, lions, or leopards. Jaguars have killed humans, but this has almost always been during a hunt when a jaguar was harassed, cornered, or wounded by hunters. Jaguars seem to be the only big cats that are not man-eaters.

Jaguars use their tails to catch fish.

This may not be completely false. Some people have seen jaguars sitting over the edge of the water scooping fish out with their paws. They noticed that the jaguar's tail would sometimes flick around on the surface of the water while it looked for fish. This movement on the surface of the water might help attract fish. In the same way, some fishers use bait on the water's surface to catch certain types of fish. It is unlikely that the jaguar uses its tail for this on purpose, but these unintentional tail movements could improve its fishing success.

Jaguars do not like to get wet.

Domestic cats have a reputation for avoiding water, but jaguars, like tigers, enjoy the water. Jaguars often cool down by lying in rivers or other bodies of water during the heat of the day. A jaguar swims very well, with its head and shoulders above the water. When it gets out of the water, it will shake its body and then each of its paws. Jaguars will cross rivers that are well over 330 feet (100 m) wide. They will even attack caimans and other large animals in the water. Jaguars will sometimes lose the tips of their tails to piranhas while they are swimming across rivers.

Jaguar Distribution in South America

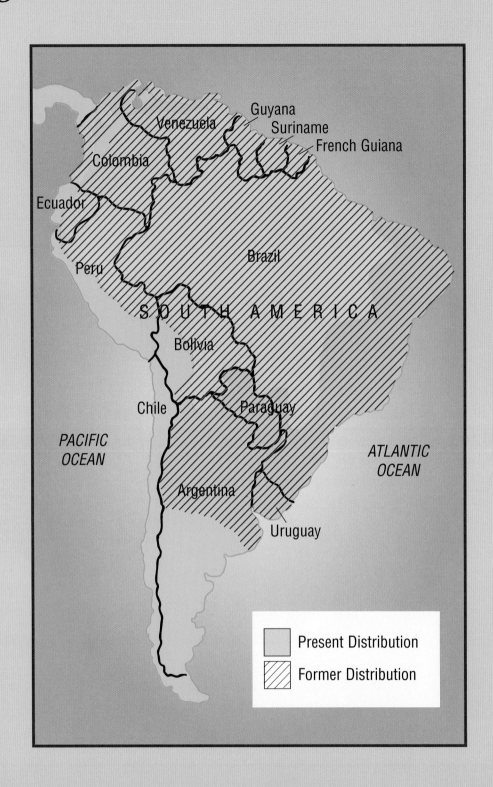

Status

Jaguars now live in only 62 percent of their former range in South America.

Until about one hundred years ago, jaguars still lived as far north as California, New Mexico, Arizona, and Texas. They could also be found in Uruguay and even farther south in Argentina. Today there are no populations of jaguars left in the United States, Uruguay, or El Salvador. In most other countries, fewer jaguars are found and only in parts of their former range. Jaguars now live in only 62 percent of their former range in South America.

Areas where jaguars live have decreased greatly in the last 100 years.

Jaguar Distribution in North and Central America

Present Distribution
Former Distribution

Decline in Population

Jaguar populations have declined because of two main reasons: hunting and habitat loss.

Hunting

Thousands of jaguars were once killed every year for their fur. Even now that most fur trading is illegal, many jaguars are hunted each year for sport and to protect livestock. In some countries where jaguars are protected by law, illegal hunting, known as **poaching**, is common. In other countries, jaguars are not even protected by law.

Jaguars are hunted by many different methods. They are often chased by specially trained dogs until they climb a tree to escape. Once in a tree, these jaguars are easy targets for the hunters.

Another common hunting technique is to wait in ambush near a jaguar's kill. Hunters also use a hollow gourd to make a noise that sounds like a jaguar. This often attracts a jaguar to the area. The hunters can kill the cat as it arrives to investigate. Some hunters leave poisoned bait for jaguars to eat.

Jaguars are still illegally hunted, but habitat loss is now their biggest threat.

Land has been cleared by slash-and-burn techniques right up to the boundary of the Cockscomb Basin Jaguar Preserve in Belize, Central America.

Habitat Loss

Today the biggest threat to jaguars is not hunting but habitat loss. Much of the jaguar's habitat is in tropical forest areas that are being destroyed. Habitat loss is often the result of an increase in the human population in a region. As the population increases, people need to clear more land on which to live. This is a problem in Central and South America, where the human population is likely to double in size approximately every 25 years.

As land is cleared for villages, crops, and livestock, jaguars are pushed into smaller and smaller areas of land. These small populations of jaguars become isolated from other jaguar populations by areas of land that are not suitable for jaguars. Jaguars cannot hunt properly in these isolated areas, and they sometimes cannot find mates. When they are seen near farms, people, or domestic animals, they can be shot.

Protecting Jaguars

In 1973 jaguars were put on Appendix 1 of the Convention on International Trade in Endangered Species of Wild Fauna and Flora (CITES). This means that the trading of jaguars or jaguar parts, such as skins, can occur only under strict regulations. It also means that commercial trading is banned. Some countries are not members of CITES and do not follow these rules. In countries such as Ecuador and Guyana, the jaguar has no legal protection. In Bolivia, hunting for trophy jaguars is allowed. In Brazil, Costa Rica, Guatemala, Mexico, and Peru, hunting is allowed only if the jaguar is considered a problem animal. A problem animal is generally one that is often seen near human populations.

Jaguars are wild animals that will never be good pets. These captive jaguars are chained to pillars all day and night.

Viewpoints

Should jaguars be destroyed if they are thought to kill livestock?

In many countries, ranchers are legally allowed to kill jaguars if they think the jaguar has killed their livestock. Some people argue that ranchers have a right to protect the animals in their care. Other people think protecting a vanishing species is more important than protecting domestic animals. They believe that ranchers often kill jaguars out of fear or to make a profit from the skin. They think that ranchers may not know which jaguar did the killing, or even if their animal was killed by a jaguar.

PRO

1 Jaguars that become cattle killers may switch completely from preying on wildlife to preying only on cattle. One jaguar was thought to have preyed on cattle one hundred times in 2 years.

2 If all jaguars that kill livestock are destroyed, there will be less conflict with humans. The remaining jaguars will not be as feared, and they will be left to live in peace.

3 Cattle should be the priority, especially in developing countries, where people urgently need the food and money that their herds produce.

CON

1 Some jaguars do prey on cattle, but many are blamed for killing cattle that they did not kill. This may happen when cattle die from other causes, such as broken legs or disease, and then the jaguar feeds on the carcass.

2 Changing ranching practices would decrease conflicts between humans and jaguars. Livestock is often allowed to roam freely throughout the forests. When cattle are confined in fenced grazing areas, jaguar attacks are rare.

3 Jaguars should be the priority, because they are decreasing in numbers throughout their range. A solution could be to pay ranchers for any cattle lost to a jaguar, as long as the rancher does not kill the jaguar.

The Fur Trade

People once killed jaguars to make their skins into fur coats. Fur trading, as it was called, became a big business in the 1960s. Since jaguars' coats are so different from one another, many skins were needed to make even one well-matched coat. Spotted cat coats were popular, and demand for them throughout Europe and North America was very high. In 1968 alone, more than 13,500 jaguar skins were brought into the United States. However, public opinion soon changed. Coats made from exotic animals that were threatened with extinction became unpopular. The CITES ban on skin trading and public pressure have helped reduce the trade in jaguar skins. Between 1976 and 1990, an average of only 117 jaguar skins a year were traded internationally. In 1990 no jaguar skins were reported to have been traded internationally. Jaguar skins continue to be traded illegally, but the total number of traded skins has been greatly reduced.

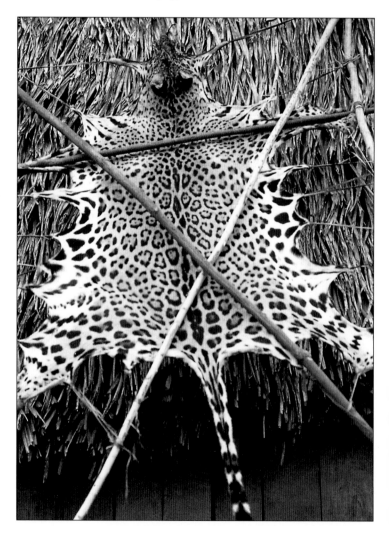

During the peak fur-trading years, thousands of jaguars were killed for fashionable coats.

The Cockscomb Basin Jaguar Preserve

In 1984 the Cockscomb Basin in Belize, Central America, became the first reserve in the world that was created especially to protect jaguars. The government of Belize, at the urging of the Belize Audubon Society and the New York Zoological Society, set aside 154 square miles (400 sq km) of territory to protect these big cats from hunting and habitat destruction.

Funding was needed to get the reserve protected, and publicity was needed to let local people know that the area was a reserve. As part of this fund-raising/publicity campaign, Melanie Watt found sponsors and rode a 144-mile (230-km) bike race in Belize. Melanie also asked the Canadian branch of the Jaguar car company, Jaguar Canada Inc., to support the reserve. The president of the car company, Mr. John Mackie, was concerned about wild

Dr. Melanie Watt rode in a 144-mile (230-km) bike race to help save the jaguars in Belize.

jaguars. Together with World Wildlife Fund Canada, he created a sponsorship package that included the Canadian, American, and British branches of the car company. They supplied $100,000 over three years to establish the Cockscomb Basin Jaguar Preserve. The area now protects jaguars, their habitat, and many other tropical forest animals. At least in this one area, jaguars have found a safe haven.

What You Can Do

You can help jaguars by learning about them and teaching others what you have learned. You can also help jaguars by becoming involved with organizations that help protect these big cats and their natural habitat. Write to one of these organizations to learn more about how they are helping jaguars. You can also ask them how you can help them protect jaguars and other wildlife.

Conservation Groups

INTERNATIONAL

World Conservation Union (IUCN)
28 rue Mauverney
CH-1196 Gland
Switzerland

World Wide Fund For Nature
Avenue du Mont Blanc
CH-1196 Gland
Switzerland

UNITED STATES

Conservation International
1015 18th St., Suite 1000
Washington, D.C.
20036

Rainforest Alliance
2 Kettle Creek
Jericho, VT
05465

Wildlife Conservation Society
185th St. and
Southern Boulevard
Bronx, NY
10460

World Wildlife Fund United States
1250 24th St. NW
Washington, D.C.
20037

CANADA

International Society for Endangered Cats Canada Inc. (ISEC)
124 Lynnbrook Rd. SE
Calgary, Alberta
T2C 1S8

World Wildlife Fund Canada
90 Eglinton Ave. E.
Suite 504
Toronto, Ontario
M4P 2Z7

Twenty Fascinating Facts

1 The jaguar is the biggest cat found in North, Central, or South America. It is the third biggest cat in the world. Only the tiger and the lion are larger.

2 Even black jaguars have spots. The black background just makes the spots very difficult to see. Because the spotting pattern is so hard to distinguish, black jaguars in captivity are often mistaken for black leopards.

3 Jaguars are now **extirpated** in the United States, El Salvador, and Uruguay.

4 Jaguars' front paws have five toes, but only four show up in their paw prints. The smaller fifth toe, or "thumb," is higher off the ground and does not leave a mark. Even though this toe is smaller, it has a well-developed retractable claw.

5 In most areas, black jaguars are very rare, but in some isolated populations, as many as one out of every three jaguars may be black.

6 Most people think that jaguars are active only at night. Research now shows that jaguars are often quite active during daylight hours as well. They even hunt during the day. Jaguars seem most active at dusk.

7 No one knows how much sleep a wild jaguar gets, but captive jaguars usually sleep about 11 hours per day.

8 The world's first protected area set aside specifically for jaguars is in Belize, Central America. One of its early sponsors was the Jaguar car company, which wanted to help protect its namesake.

9 The name "jaguar" may have come from *yaguara*, which in the Tupi-Guarani language means "wild beast that overcomes its prey at a bound." The jaguar has many other names. One of its most common names is *el tigre*, which means "the tiger" in Spanish.

10 Jaguars love the water. They often swim or just lie in the water to cool off. Many of the jaguar's prey, such as capybaras, caimans, and turtles, are also water lovers.

11 When a jaguar eats its prey, it often eats many bones and claws as well. One reason it does not puncture its intestines with these sharp objects is because of all the fur it also eats. The fur gets wrapped around the sharp pieces, protecting the stomach and intestines of the big cat.

12 Jaguars have extremely powerful jaws. They can easily break through large bones and turtle shells. Their rough tongue can be used to get meat off their prey's bones. It is also used to clean their own fur.

13 Jaguars and cougars are often found in the same countries. They seem to avoid one another because of their preferred habitats. Jaguars are usually found in areas with lots of water, while cougars tend to prefer higher, drier ground. Jaguars have been known to attack and kill cougars, but this is very rare.

14 Adult jaguars spend almost their entire lives alone. They usually contact others of their own species only to mate or when raising their young.

18 Jaguars are powerful predators, but even they may be wounded or killed by their prey. They are also preyed upon by external parasites, such as ticks, and intestinal parasites, such as hookworms. They also may get sick from illnesses such as rabies and feline leukemia.

19 Scrape marks are thought to be a form of jaguar communication. Very small scrapes are sometimes found beside larger ones. This suggests that scraping is one of the skills a mother teaches her young cubs.

20 In captivity, jaguars can live to be well over 20 years old. In the wild, where conditions are more difficult, most jaguars do not live past 12 years old.

15 Although jaguars are territorial, young males sometimes travel long distances from their places of birth. This is likely because male jaguars will not usually be tolerated in the home range of another male jaguar. The young male must keep moving through other jaguar territories until he finds a territory of his own.

16 Jaguars do not make good pets. Even friendly, hand-raised cubs are dangerous once they become adults.

17 Jaguars are silent hunters. They quietly stalk and then leap from cover to pounce on their unsuspecting prey.

Glossary

caiman: A large reptile that is closely related to the alligator. Jaguars prey on several different species of caimans both in and out of the water.

carnivores: Animals that eat mainly the flesh and body parts of other animals

domestic animals: Animals that have been tamed for the benefit of humans. Examples of domestic animals include cats and dogs, cows, horses, and sheep.

extirpated: A species that no longer exists in a certain area, but may be found somewhere else

gestation period: The length of time a female is pregnant with young

home range: The entire area in which an individual jaguar lives

melanistic: A jaguar that has black fur. Melanistic jaguars have the same spotted pattern as golden jaguars, but the pattern is harder to see on a black background.

opportunistic feeders: Animals that do not wait for specific things to eat, but instead eat whatever prey they come across

poaching: A type of hunting that is not legal. Animals are often poached for their body parts, which are then sold illegally.

retractable claws: Claws that can be pulled back into the paw when not in use. Most cats have retractable claws, but dogs have nonretractable claws that are permanently in an outstretched position.

rosettes: The black-outlined circles on a jaguar's fur

scat: An animal fecal dropping

scent marks: Areas where an animal urinates to let other animals know it is in the area

scrape: A possible form of cat communication, where a cat makes a scratching mark on the ground with its back feet

Suggested Reading

Alderton, David. *Wild Cats of the World*. London: Blandford, 1993.

Guggisberg, C.A.W. *Wild Cats of the World*. New York: Taplinger Publishing, 1975.

Hoogesteijn, Rafael and Mondolfi, Edgardo. *The Jaguar*. Caracas, Venezuela: Armitano Publishers, 1992.

Lumpkin, Susan. *Big Cats*. New York: Facts on File, 1993.

Nowell, Kristin and Jackson, Peter. *Status Survey and Conservation Action Plan: Wild Cats*. Switzerland: International Union for Conservation of Nature and Natural Resources, 1996.

Watt, Melanie. *Jaguar Woman*. Toronto: Key Porter Books, 1989.

Index